THIS HANDBOOK BELONGS TO:

_____

I became a Tomboy on this Date _____.

I belong to the _____ Tribe.

I Stomped Up on this Date _____.

My Personal Tribal Name is

_____.

I took the ❑ Warrior Path ❑ Mistress Path

on this Date _____.

BADGES I HAVE EARNED

Your Home and Family   Date Earned

❑ Love & Marriage   _____

❑ Cooking & Dining   _____

❑ House & Garden   _____

❑ Happy Family   _____

❑ Building & Tool Usage   ___   ___

D1433002

BADGES I HAVE EARNED

You and Your Community	Date Earned
❏ Activism & Your Community	_____
❏ Social Director	_____
❏ Sports	_____
❏ Party!	_____
❏ "Herstory" & Your Place in It	_____
❏ Coming Out	_____

The World Around You	
❏ Nature	_____
❏ The Beasts & the Children	_____
❏ The Garden	_____
❏ Hiking	_____
❏ Camping	_____
❏ Outdoor Activities	_____

Living Well	
❏ Picknicking	_____
❏ Spirituality	_____
❏ Making a Fashion Statement	_____
❏ Vacationing	_____
❏ To Your Very Good Health	_____
❏ Arts & Music	_____
❏ Reading	_____

AMAZON

GIRLS

HANDBOOK

AMAZON

GIRLS

HANDBOOK

Becky Thacker

Illustrations by Anne Leuck Feldhaus

Wicker Park Press

Chicago

Published in 2002 by
Wicker Park Press, Ltd.
1801 West Byron
Suite 1C
Chicago, Illinois 60613

Printed in the U.S.A.

Library of Congress Cataloging-in-Publication Data

Thacker, Becky.
  Amazon Girls handbook / Becky Thacker.
    p. cm.
  ISBN 0-89733-508-2
  1. Lesbians—Recreation—Handbooks, manuals, etc. 2. Outdoor
recreation—Handbooks, manuals, etc. 3. Amazon Girls
(Organization)—Handbooks, manuals, etc. I. Title.
  GV183.2 .T53 2002
  790'.86'643--dc21
                                                    2002003926

For my mom, who always said, "It never hurt anybody to learn how to make a good white sauce," and for Harriet, whom I love extravagantly.

CONTENTS

INTRODUCTION 11

WHAT WE ARE 13

THE SPIRIT OF AMAZON GIRLS

The Motto 17
The Salute 17
Amazon Girl Ideals 18
The Sacred Amazon Girl Oath 18
Your Badge 19
Your Uniform 19

WHAT AMAZON GIRLS DO 21

UPWARD TO GODDESS
Rank Requirements

Tomboy 23
Amazon 26
Warrior 28
Mistress 29
Matriarch 30
Goddess 31

BADGE REQUIREMENTS

Preface 33
The Badges 34–35

YOUR HOME AND FAMILY

Love and Marriage 39
Cooking and Dining 43
House and Garden 47
Happy Family 49
Building and Tool Usage 53

YOU AND YOUR COMMUNITY

Activism and Supporting Your Community 59
Social Director 61
Sports 63
Party! 65
"Herstory" and Your Place In It 67
Coming Out 69

THE WORLD AROUND YOU

Nature 73
The Beasts and the Children 75
The Garden 77
Hiking 79
Camping 85
Outdoor Activities 89

LIVING WELL

Picnicking 99
Spirituality 103
Making a Fashion Statement 105
Vacationing 107
To Your Very Good Health 109
Arts & Music 111
Reading 113

AMAZON GIRLS IN ACTION

Where Do We Begin? And Other FAQs 117
Sample Flyer/Sign-Up Sheet 121
Amazon Girls on the Road 123
Your Life as an Amazon Girl 141

SOURCES FOR YOUNG AND OLD AMAZON GIRLS 143

INTRODUCTION

How many of us desperately wanted to be scouts when we were kids? We sat there in third grade, lumpish in the dresses and penny loafers our moms had selected for us, and daydreamed of strong, stalwart alter egos. Dressed in khaki uniforms with many snap-closed pockets (Note to younger candidates: this was before Velcro), fire-starting badges stitched onto our sleeves by admiring, also imaginary, girlfriends, we strode along unblazed trails, unafraid of marauding snakes, spiders, or jaguars (Note to Y.C.: this was before serial killers also), followed by our troop of handsome butch pals.

In our dreams, we pitched cozy, two-person tents and unrolled our bedrolls next to our faithful best pals. Our troop leader, who strongly resembled that gym teacher we loved so much, regularly had to be rescued by us from marauding s, s and js (see above). We sat around the campfire at night and looked modest as the members of our troop praised our wisdom and bravery. Sure we did. You remember. Admit it.

Yeah yeah yeah, and instead our moms signed us up for Brownies and we ate cookies, drank Kool-Aid, sang some dippy songs in a circle of wheezing, myopic, homely little twits in those dumb brown dresses, and went home to dream our lonely dreams.

Sure, a few of our friends say they were in wonderful Scout troops and did most of the things many of us only dreamed of doing. They were the lucky ones. You probably were not, or you wouldn't be reading this now.

Fear not! It's never to late to realize your dreams. You have a few really good friends now, don't you? Middleaged, cranky, flat-footed and weary they may be, but under those tired paunches beat the youthful hearts of fellow adventurers, yes? Ah hah!

So gather your friends around you. Don your uniforms, lift your graying heads proudly, and raise your staffs high. Give one another the special salute and set off down the trail. Welcome to the organization called the Amazon Girls!

WHAT WE ARE

Amazon Girls is a community of out, proud lesbians who seek adventure, whimsy and the rekindling of ancient dreams. We want to be all that we can be, without the necessity of joining some Don't Ask Don't Tell military organization or becoming counselors at a children's camp. The Amazon Girls community has a structure; members can find their places within their tribes and villages and advance through the ranks or not, as they choose.

Younger candidates will find that most of the activities in this handbook will apply to them as well. Much younger candidates, fear not! The Amazon Teen Handbook is in the works. In the meantime, know that nobody, regardless of age, race, dietary preferences, or affectional preference is prohibited from being an Amazon Girl. You will merely need to adapt some of the activities to your personal situation, and fortunately, an Amazon Girl is indeed adaptable.

THE TRIBE

The smallest unit of Amazon Girls is your tribe. A tribe may consist of five to eight members and will function much like your typical dysfunctional family except you're all lesbians awash with unrealized ideals, and participation is strictly voluntary.

Your tribe will have a name that should reflect the personality of the group as a whole, or what you'd like to personify. You will want to think carefully about selecting a name for your tribe; remember, you're stuck with it and you don't want a persona that's impossible to live up to— or live down to. We've heard of a legendary tribe of nostalgic former ballplayers who called their tribe the Bar Dykes. Their hikes never go very far—twelve steps and they all have to sit down and process. You may name your tribe after a historical figure, a bird or animal, or even a contemporary figure you admire.

THE VILLAGE

As your community forms more tribes of Amazon Girls, you'll need a larger group to help organize activities and throw some really big potlucks. Please don't call it an umbrella group. Call it your village. Imagine large fields of dome (or OK, umbrella) tents, a little like a festival but with better food and everyone knows everyone else's first name most of the time. Your village should contain four to five tribes at the most, and should meet once or twice a year if possible, with food, of course.

MOVING THROUGH THE RANKS

You've been holding your breath waiting for this part, haven't you, you rascal? Yes, you can indeed earn Amazon

Girl badges for your accomplishments. Earn enough badges and devote enough energy to this project, and you can gain rank and status in your village. You can schedule little awards ceremonies, which are a good excuse to break open that special bottle of Chardonnay you've been hoarding. Sappy little Tomboys will gaze at you in awe and offer to carry your backpack for you. (Don't tell your partner about this.)

You and your tribe can work on badges together. It'll be fun, you'll learn things, and while sometimes you'll feel like an utter idiot engaging in such regressive behavior, deep down inside you'll be pleased as punch at your own talents.

When you first join Amazon Girls, you will go through a probationary period. As you learn the ideals, the salute, the essentials of what's involved with being an Amazon Girl, you'll be referred to as a Tomboy. Relax, it's just part of that bonding/initiation rite thing that humans love so dearly, sick, isn't it? You'll have a Tomboy pin to put on your uniform and wear during your probationary period as an Amazon Girl. Cool, huh?

STOMPING UP

You will graduate ("Stomp up") to Amazon after three months as a Tomboy and after you demonstrate knowledge of the Amazon Girl oath, salute, and motto, and some basic skills. As you earn badges and awards, you may eventually achieve the status of Warrior or Mistress, depend-

ing on your mood, then Matriarch or even, if you devote
your life to this, Goddess.

THE SPIRIT OF AMAZON GIRLS

THE MOTTO

The Amazon Girls motto is, "We're prepared for a few things."

This means that whatever unexpected situation comes up in your life, you'll try to manage it with grace, skill, tact, and aplomb, or at least find a friend to help you hide the body.

THE SALUTE

The Amazon Girls salute is simple. A brief practice session before the mirror will help you perfect it. Stand up (or at least sit up straight, for heaven's sake, didn't your mom teach you anything?), shoulders back, eyes front. Raise your right hand, striking yourself in the middle of the forehead with the palm of your hand. Roll your eyes heavenward at the same time. Excellent! Now practice with a friend.

You will be expected to give this salute whenever special salutes are appropriate.

AMAZON GIRL IDEALS

You will want to learn these by heart so you may live in the true spirit of early Amazon Girls:

An Amazon Girl is attuned to Mom Nature
and Mom Earth.
An Amazon Girl is brave.
An Amazon Girl is whimsical.
An Amazon Girl is adaptable.
An Amazon Girl is hungry.
An Amazon Girl is probably broke, but
nearly always generous.

THE SACRED AMAZON GIRL OATH

As an Amazon Girl I promise to always try to be out and proud, to be kind to the beasts, the children, and the very old, to live the good life, and never to sweat the small stuff.

YOUR BADGE

The Amazon Girl badge symbolizes several essential concepts of Amazon Girl life. The round part symbolizes the planet earth, or as we call it, home. The wide-flowing blue line down the center stands for the longest river in the world, which is not the Wabash. The plus sign at the bottom indicates the generally ovarian nature of the organization.

YOUR UNIFORM

The technical term for your Amazon Girl uniform is "your outfit." The basic outfit will consist of, and don't you dare snicker, a top and a bottom.

Tops may include blue denim work shirt, khaki shirt with many snap or Velcro pockets, or plain t-shirts or sweatshirts of a color your tribe agrees on.

Bottoms may include blue jeans, khaki pants with many snap or Velcro pockets, or if you're a Mistress, a basic little black dress.

Badges should be stitched onto your uniform top, unless your tribe agrees to invest in nifty matching backpacks to display them. Mistresses may place their badges wherever they choose.

Optional equipment:

Shoes: Sensible walking shoes, hiking boots or if you're a Mistress, come-f*-me pumps.

Nifty matching backpacks.

Swiss army knives.

Water bottle in shoulder carrier as designed by Tupperware™.

Anything else that your tribe deems appropriate, such as nifty vests or headgear.

WHAT AMAZON GIRLS DO

Amazon Girls do whatever they want to do. Preferred activities will probably include the things you were discouraged from doing as a child and young woman: hiking, camping, drinking red wines with fish and poultry, flying kites, singing raucously on full moon nights, and getting really sweaty in the garden and doing other activities you really, really, really enjoy. Really.

As a tribe you will want to attend community events such as concerts, festivals, and Take Back the Night rallies. You will want to plan and consume elaborate picnic meals at outdoor symphonies, go camping or take weekend trips to interesting places, throw parties, and go to shows.

If you really want to take this thing seriously, you and your tribe will also try to do some good in your communities. In fact, regular community service is a requirement for both Matriarch and Goddess ranks.

UPWARD TO GODDESS

MY PATH TO GODDESS

If you choose to make Amazon Girls a driving force in your life, and why not, there are worse hobbies to have, you will plan to work your way through the ranks, earning badges and performing activities that improve the quality of your life and/or the lives of others around you. Earning badges will teach you new abilities and enhance the ones you already have. You'll be a good example for those who follow you. You'll have a really swell time.

RANK REQUIREMENTS

TOMBOY

To be a Tomboy, you need only express a willingness to live your life according to the Amazon Girl ideals. You'll demonstrate this willingness by learning the Amazon Girl oath, the motto, salute, and ideals. Each day you'll perform one act of moral will, however minor. This will help you develop the fortitude you'll need to be out and proud, and to be able to tell your loved ones, without snickering, "I am a Tomboy."

The Tomboy pin is much like the Amazon Girl patch, except that there's more pink on it. The reason for this is much the same as the rationale behind the "Boy Named Sue" song. If you don't remember it, ask one of your elders. It's one of those sick "toughen you up" things. Don't expect too much of this in Amazon Girls, however.

If your tribe is really into the control and power thing, you may have further requirements inflicted on you by the higher-ranking members, at least until they tire of the heady rush of having someone besides their dogs to order around. You may have to start the fire for the marshmallow roasts, send all the party invitations, or make all the phone calls for an event. It's good practice, and gives you incentive to work on your Amazon rank requirements. Remind your tribe that they're not allowed to touch your person. (Unless you want them to, of course.) This isn't like that male-dominated quasi-military organization where they do S/M things to each other in the name of "initiation." Honest.

Oh. Act of moral will? It means going ahead and doing something positive that's hard for you to do. It may mean taking the trash out when your feet hurt, or shutting up and letting your sweetie tell you what an awful day she's had without interrupting her with "You think *you've* got problems." It might mean turning in that nifty Swiss Army knife with 17 blades and attachments that you found in the Porta-Jane to Festival Headquarters, or refraining from whispering to your friend during a concert, "Gawd, this chorus sucks canal water."

It might mean doing some niggling unimportant little task that you've been putting off because it seems incredibly trivial, or it may mean refraining from doing some niggling unimportant little task when you should be sitting quietly watching the sunset.

Performing an act of moral will daily helps you eventually develop self-control and virtue, the way one develops a long-neglected muscle. It could also make you unbearably smug, so watch it. It also can get to be addictive.

Soon you'll have to refrain from doing a moral act as your moral act, and won't that be confusing?

There's no statute of limitations on this duty, by the way. Amazons, Warriors and Mistresses both, Matriarchs and Goddesses are also expected to perform this. It will be easier for them; they've been doing it for a long time anyway.

AMAZON

In order to qualify for Amazon status you will need to know the Amazon Girl oath, salute, ideals, and motto. You will also need to demonstrate your ability to do the following:

- ☑ Prepare a meal that is edible, fills up the diners and doesn't make them throw up.

- ☑ Perform one:
  - a: row a boat
  - b: drive a stick shift
  - c: ride a horse
  - d. drive a motorcycle.

- ❏ Correctly identify two local birds and three wildflowers.

- ☑ Describe one:
  - a: Lesbian Connection
  - b: Kate Clinton
  - c: NWMF
  - d. Naiad Press
  - e: Provincetown

❑ Arrange your sleeping quarters in a way that
   is inviting, relaxing, and/or sexy.

When you "Stomp Up" to being a full-fledged Amazon, you'll be expected to participate in tribal and village
activities. You should act as if you enjoy them. If you don't
enjoy any of them, it's probably an indication you've been
sitting around on your tush expecting everyone else to plan
and organize activities. No wonder you're not having any
fun in your life, you grouch, you've been a follower and a
taker for too damn long. What's the matter with you? Stand
up straight. Stop whining. Go fly a kite (see Outdoor Activities badge).

Your "Stomping Up" ceremony can be as elaborate or
as simple as your tribe cares to make it. If you still have
some of that really ripe Brie left from your last party, this
would probably be a good time to get a fresh box of Triscuits
to go with it, and maybe some fresh grapes. A little smoked
salmon? Oh, and everyone should recite the Amazon Girl
oath and maybe give the salute.

But we digress. Now that you're an Amazon, you're
entitled to start earning badges. You will get to speak up at
meetings and suggest activities. Your life will be thrilling,
fulfilling, and rich, or at least no worse than it was before.

PATH CHOICE (WARRIOR/MISTRESS)

You may select a specific path to follow at this point, depending on your personality, inclinations, and daydreams.
If your interests lie in the social and decorating areas, you

may have Mistress tendencies. If you'd rather get dirty and grubby in the outdoors, Warrior is the path for you. If your heart goes pit-a-pat over a number of different subjects, you may not want to select a path at all. The only drawback to this is deciding what to wear.

WARRIOR

A warrior is an Amazon Girl who is frequently called "sir" by unseeing clerks and waitpersons. She knows that "packing" means more than just filling a suitcase. A true warrior can make feminine hearts flutter simply by grimacing into a strong wind. Or would like to.

Warrior Patch Requirements:
   ❑ Earn two of the following badges:
      Building and Tool Usage, Sports, The Garden, Camping, Hiking, Outdoor Activities

❑ Study the style and moves of one of these social icons to be sure you understand the concept of "cool": James Dean, k.d. lang, Margarethe Cammemeyer

❑ At your next dyke public event, put the moves to work as you stand in the parking lot or lobby and pose. Deduct two points each if you need to use a lit cigarette or mirrored sunglasses as part of the effect.

MISTRESS

A mistress goes where she likes, does what she pleases, and takes no prisoners. Black leather bustier is optional.

Mistress Patch Requirements:
❑ Earn two of the following badges:
Party!, Cooking and Dining, Decorator Badge, Making a Fashion Statement, Arts and Music

❑ Using the force of your personal magnetism, inspire three different women to ask you out (don't tell your sweetie).

❑ Turn them down.

After you have been a full-fledged Amazon for a while, you may wish to work toward a higher status in your tribe. To do this, you'll be expected to earn badges, socialize a bit, help others a bit, and prove yourself to be other than a self-centered, hedonistic consumer except at appropriate times.

MATRIARCH

This rank is something all serious Amazon Girls will strive for, though not all will reach the goal. People will recognize you in public places. Tomboys and Amazons will come to you for advice. You're not allowed to charge for this.

To achieve this rank, you will need to earn twelve badges (at least two in each of the major categories) plus accomplish at least four:

❑ Be selected as a tribal leader.

❑ Arrange at least two campouts, boating trips, or 2+ hour hikes that actually occur.

❑ Host at least two dinners for four or more people, for at least twenty-four hours after which nobody becomes ill or stops speaking to you.

❑ Attend at least one commitment ceremony as an invited guest even if you have to shamelessly wheedle for an invitation from someone who never liked you that much, nor you her.

❑ Belong to a softball team for at least one season even if you don't actually play.

❑ Be a dues-paying member of NOW, PFLAG, HRC, HSUS, Greenpeace, or NAACP.

GODDESS

This rank is achieved by very few women in any community, and is not for the faint of heart. It acknowledges those rare women who truly personify all the ideals of the Amazon Girls, and gives the rest of us something to aspire to. The award itself is a small Venus of Willendorf insignia, worn next to the proud and weary heart.

To achieve this rank, you will need to earn fifteen badges (at least two in each of the major categories) plus be unabashedly out to your family, your friends, and your workplace, plus accomplish one of the below:

❑ Organize a major community event such as a concert or fundraiser.

❑ Open and maintain a community center or business such as a bookstore, recording company or coffee house.

❏ Serve on the board of a major local organization (chorus pride, or festival board) for at least
one year.

❏ Get arrested at a NOW or Lesbian Avengers
event.

❏ Be interviewed on local TV speaking about a
major gay or women's issue.

❏ Serve as president or facilitator for a support,
discussion, or CR group for at least one year.

❏ Serve on a speaker's board for at least one year.

❏ And accomplish two of the below:
Host a pitch-in.
Write a letter to LC.
Spend a day staffing a booth at a pride event or
festival.
Present a workshop at a pride event or festival.
Correspond with a pen pal from another culture
for at least three months.

BADGE REQUIREMENTS

PREFACE

Those of you who decide to embrace the Amazon Girls philosophy and way of life wholeheartedly will commence earning badges enthusiastically. Others of you, with a more modern bent, will immediately start figuring out how to collect as many badges as possible without completing any of the requirements. Unlike certain quasi-military organizations which purport to build character, Amazon Girls is concerned with giving you already-formed characters a home. If you want to live in your home as a scummy, cheating low-life creep, that's certainly your prerogative. But nobody will invite you to her parties if you're going through life as a collector. Be warned.

Being adults, you should by now have a modicum of common sense. Some badge requirements, for example, don't lend themselves to repetition. If you came out to your mom twenty years ago, or closed your community-centered business a year ago, it would be ridiculous to say "I can't go through that again" and not count your previous experience toward the requirement. On the other hand, just because you went camping once as a child doesn't relieve you of the need to camp out in order to earn your Camping badge.

There's a little check box before each requirement for you to record the date you've completed that requirement. If you'd rather put a happy-face or other personal signal on the box of completed requirements, feel free.

So, badge-earners, you're on your honor here. When you deem, in good conscience, that you've completed your requirements for a badge, notify National Headquarters (aka the author) by sending in your particulars, which include name, address with zip, badge earned, any stories and comments about your experiences earning it, and feel free to include cookies, as long as they contain no raisins and your hands were clean when you handled them. Oh, and include $2.50 or whatever you can afford to cover our expenses, you think postage charges are dropping?

The badges are fabric leaf-shapes in the colors as shown after each badge description. Stitched (or glued) onto your outfits in fine array, they will look most impressive. Trust us, as we trust you.

THE BADGES

Your Home and Family
Love and Marriage [*green*]
Cooking and Dining [*blue*]
House and Garden [*yellow*]
Happy Family [*red*]
Building and Tool Usage [*orange*]

briar leaf

You and Your Community
Activism & Supporting Your Community [*green*]
Social Director [*blue*]
Sports [*yellow*]
Party! [*red*]
'Herstory' and Your Place In It [*orange*]
Coming Out [*purple*]

cherry leaf

The World Around You
Nature [*green*]
The Beasts and the Children [*blue*]
The Garden [*yellow*]
Hiking [*red*]
Camping [*orange*]
Outdoor Activities [*purple*]

maple leaf

Living Well
Picnicking [*green*]
Spirituality [*blue*]
Making a Fashion Statement [*yellow*]
Vacationing [*red*]
To Your Very Good Health [*orange*]
Arts & Music [*purple*]
Reading [*pink*]

oak leaf

briar leaf

YOUR HOME AND FAMILY

Here's where you live. If it's comfortable and happy, you're likely to function well in your community and your planet. Your home doesn't need to be a mansion to serve you well; it's what you do with the space around you that matters. Your family may be large or small, including partner, roommates, friends and those who depend on you, such as kids, pets, houseplants and the birds you feed. Care for them with love; include light, color, and peace in your surroundings, get enough roughage in your diet, and you'll have a solid foundation for good living.

Your family will have its own way of doing things, its own traditions and pastimes. Don't ever let anyone else tell you what should work for your family.

green

LOVE AND MARRIAGE

" **A**fter sex and money, temperature is the biggest source of conflict for couples. Housekeeping you can always hire out, but temperature you just can't."

—Overheard in a public restroom.

This badge may be earned by any of you who would like to live happily ever after with a sweetie at your side. Perform all of these:

☑ Select a happily married couple to serve as your model for relationships. This could be any couple you have observed on a regular basis, from grandparents to your best friends. If you can only think of a couple in a favorite work of fiction or a TV show, probably you'd benefit more by living for two years in healthier circles than by trying to earn this badge just now.

❑ Write at least one journal page for each of the following subjects, based on how your couple:
    Settles disagreements
    Shares responsibilities
    Shows affection for each other
    Shares minutiae of daily life, such as meals, rituals, finances, visits.

❑ Read at least one book or series of articles on establishing healthy relationships. Make a note of three ideas or suggestions you think would be helpful for a couple to know, and discuss these with your tribe or your sweetie.

❑ Perform at least two works of activism to further the possibility of governmental same-sex marriage recognition. This can be a phone call or letter to lawmaker, a speech to your church, civic group or college class, letters to papers, or something more creative.

❑ Make a list of ten qualities you'd like a mate to have.

❑ Put a checkmark next to those qualities you possess yourself. Well, I should think you would be embarrassed. Maybe that's why your last three relationships fizzled. (Just kidding, dearest.)

❑ If you have a sweetie, put a star next to those qualities she possesses. Tell her about them.

❑ Share information with your tribe about magazine articles or web pages concerning same-sex marriage.

Do one of the following:

❑ Do some special loving thing for your sweetie, such as a massage, special meal, flowers, or a household chore she hates to do. If you have no current sweetie, write a journal page about doing this for an imaginary sweetie.

❑ Plan an imaginary wedding. Be sure to include location, setting, who you'd invite, dress, music, and any special words you'd like to include in your ceremony.

blue

COOKING AND DINING

There are a lot of requirements for this badge, and you'll enjoy every bite. To earn this badge, perform all of these:

❏ If you are not an experienced cook, read the chapter in *Joy of Cooking*, or another mainstream cookbook, about safe handling of foods so you won't poison yourself or anyone else by accident. (Note to Mistresses: if you actually intend to poison a mouthy ex, don't try to blame these badge requirements for it. You don't fool us for one second.)

❑ List four sources of protein, including at least two that you could serve to your vegan friends. If you don't know what a vegan is, ask your friends. If you take up cooking regularly, sooner or later you'll have one over for dinner.

❑ Go to the produce section of your local grocery. Purchase some of those mysterious tubers and fruits with the express purpose of consuming them with the gusto of a hound dog. You may also plan other activities with them, but that's another merit badge.

❑ Find a copy of the food groups pyramid. You know, the one with carbohydrates at the bottom and fats at the top. Study this until you understand it. Use it faithfully in the next few requirements:

❑ Plan dinner menus for the next four nights. The meals should incorporate good nutrition, include at least two servings of fresh fruits or veggies, and not be repulsive in appearance. Don't get too grandiose here, because the next step is probably already obvious to you.

❑ Prepare each of these meals. Feel free to refer to cookbooks as needed, and/or to consult any friends who cook if you're unsure of any procedures.

☑ Set your table attractively. Include candles, cloth napkins, flowers, a flat bowl of colored rocks or greenery to add visual appeal. If your dishes and flatware don't already match, exercise some discretion in how you blend them on your table.

❏ Invite a friend or sweetie to join you for at least one of these meals:

Do not turn on the television, radio, or read during these meals. If you have a dining companion, converse pleasantly with him/her/it. If not, ponder some subject (besides revenge) that is pleasant to you.

If you have leftovers, take them to work the next day for lunch. Your co-workers will be so impressed.

❏ Locate and investigate at least two new restaurants in your area. Report to your tribe about menu selections, price range, appearance of the places, and directions to them.

❏ Have a meal at one of these restaurants. Again, report to your tribe about the experience. Tell what you ate, how it was, how the service and comfort level were, and whether you'd like to go there again. If your tribe accompanied you to this restaurant already, report anyway. It'll be a good exercise in reality vs. perception.

❑ Identify at least five non-commercial flavorings; these may include commercially packaged herbs and fruit juices, but not preparations such as A-1 Sauce.

And remember kids, always remember the diner's mantra: "I'll practice safe eating and always use a condiment every time I eat."

yellow

HOUSE AND GARDEN

"And no putting dirty dishes in the drainer."
Creating a happy home can be a life-long process. While many view homemaking as a dismal chore, doing this at least part-time can enhance your life if you approach it as an artist approaches her vision. To earn this badge, perform five of the following:

- ❑ Draw a floor plan of your dream house. Make a list of ways your present house is similar to this. Make a list of ways your present house differs from this.

- ❑ Devise a means of changing one of those differences. Make a note of reasons why you haven't made such a change, such as space limitations, finances, or inertia.

- ❑ Draw a layout of your current yard, garden, or patio. Would you change this layout? How so?

❑ Invite a gardening pal to your home for a meal and a tour of your estate. Calm down, you can always order a pizza. The point of this is to make a note of her/his impressions, what gets praised, what suggestions are made.

❑ Spend an afternoon tidying up your yard/patio. Throw out trash; rake up leaves and debris, repair broken fence pickets. Spend at least a few minutes admiring the results.

❑ Fix up one problem area inside your house. For example, rearrange a cluttered closet or corner, paint or paper an ugly wall, or rearrange your living room furniture in a way that invites guests to come in and settle.

❑ Buy yourself a new mop. If your budget allows, also get a nice new pair of garden gloves, a shovel, or a watering can.

❑ Go to your local fabric shop and buy a couple of yards of material that suits your fancy. Cut and hem napkins from this material. If you lack a sewing machine, get some iron-on hemming stuff.

❑ From items you've collected on your last vacation (shells, driftwood, whatever), fashion yourself a pair of napkin rings or a candleholder for your table. Trot these out next time you have company. Accept adulation graciously.

red

HAPPY FAMILY; MAKING TIME FOR WHAT'S IMPORTANT

Call us dogmatic if you will, but Amazon Girls think that if you don't have time to earn this badge, you really don't have time to have a family. In that case, Amazon Girls suggests you work on your priorities. Your family may include your sweetie or spouse, dependent children, or critters, but it will be generally more fun if you have humans to relate to, at least for this badge. If you don't have humans in your family, we're sure you can apply the concepts creatively to Furball, Binky and Sh*t-for-Brains. To earn this badge, perform all of the following:

If you have a human family, for the next two months:

❑ Arrange to have at least five meals each week as a family, at a table, with no distractions. Try to ensure that most of the food is shared, rather than person A having a burger, person B having a salad, and person C eating ice cream. Talk to one another about topics you don't usually discuss.

❑ Go with your family to the library, where each of you checks out a different book of interest. Take turns discussing your respective books at family meals.

❑ Take a walk once a week with your family. Pay attention to your surroundings, and share your sights and impressions with one another.

❑ Have a family portrait taken during this time. This needn't be professional; a friend with a camera will suffice. Plan and arrange your picture to express your family's unique qualities; feel free to use costumes or props if you wish. Provide each family member with a copy of this photo.

If you have a spouse, for the next two months:

❑ Arrange to go out alone with your spouse at least one evening a month. Spend the time discussing why you like each other so much, and planning your next date.

Tell your spouse at least once a day that you love her. Not that perfunctory "Pass the saltIloveyou" thing you've been doing lately, but a really mushy smoldering declaration.

❑ Remove the television from its position as honored guest in the living room; move it to a room you hardly ever go to, and turn it on only when you have a specific need to see something. Then turn it off immediately afterwards.

❑ Make a serious effort to curb critical thoughts of family members, even if they are thoughtless selfish creeps who never even put the dishes away when it's their turn.

orange

BUILDING AND TOOL USAGE

Imagine that you and your tribe have rented, sight un-seen, for an entire week, a romantic cottage at a remote location by the sea. "Magical! You'll lose all ambition when you walk in the door!" the brochure says. You arrive late on a Saturday night, tired and hungry, to discover that the cottage is a bleak and shoddy hovel. Further, imagine that the Pit of Horrors is equipped with only the most primi-tive of cooking implements and household tools, so that you frequently have to improvise each by using its oppo-site number.

Since this has happened to most people who like ad-venture and are over thirty, it should be an easy exercise. In fact, it's the stuff of way too many heterosexual "comic romance" movies. Fortunately, Amazon Girls are hardy and adaptable women who are able to earn this badge in their sleep, by doing three of the tasks below:

❑ Perform one of these:

a. Demonstrate two ways to improvise serving implements at a potluck when nobody remembered to bring any, or

b. one way to serve hot soup at a potluck when nobody remembered a ladle. Award yourself extra points if the device can reach those tiny carrots at the bottom of the pot, or

c. a non-commercial means of dismantling and consuming a lobster or an artichoke.

❑ Build a barricade that will actually keep a cat, a healthy young dog, or a two-year-old human out of a room for a whole day.

❑ Cut and stack enough firewood and kindling for two campfires without injury to yourself or your fellow campers.

❑ Design and build two of the following or something useful of similar difficulty:

A table that will hold a full meal without collapsing.

A stairway railing for the rickety ladder steps into the "romantic" but unlit sleeping loft that your sweetie is too short and round to get up to without help.

A lampshade for the bare bulb over the kitchen table that is the only form of illumination in the kitchen and makes everyone look like a dead fish.

Before...   After

A window covering that will prevent the neighbors from seeing into a window that's at least 2' x 3', which will not fall down in the throes of passion (the covering, not the window—if the window falls down in the throes of passion, see me later).

Something to sit on at an outdoor festival that will prevent chiggers, locked knees, or a slipped disk.

A shelf to hold all the detritus you collected on your last vacation.

cherry leaf

YOU AND YOUR COMMUNITY

Here's another street where you live. A true Amazon Girl does whatever she can to help her community to be strong, active, and a fun place to hang out. We all know people who sit back and wait for someone else to organize an event, group, or business, then criticize her for not doing it the way they would have. Make a point to earn your place in your community as you earn these badges, thereby enriching your own life and the lives of those around you.

/ green

ACTIVISM AND SUPPORTING
YOUR COMMUNITY

I t's not absolutely necessary to get arrested as you earn
this badge, though that would give you a certain panache
in the eyes of your comrades. To earn this badge, perform
five of the following:

☑ Try to shop at festival craft areas and indepen-
dently owned businesses whenever possible.
You'd be surprised what creative holiday shopping can be done this way.

☑ Subscribe to at least one gay or lesbian publication. Read most of the articles and ads in each
issue.

☑ If you have a computer, subscribe to (or lurk
regularly in) a gay or lesbian news group. Refrain from joining in on flame wars.

❑ Attend at least four committee meetings, planning, support, or discussion groups in the next

year. Try to maintain a role of peacemaker in any disputes, or at least refrain from throwing gasoline on the flames when the two community prima donnas begin to rehash their personal grievances again.

☑ Support young people by doing one of these:
Joining PFLAG.
Advise or counsel a youth group.
Write your local school board about safe schools.
Moderate a computer news group or chat room
    where youngsters may discuss their issues.
Contribute regularly to such a news group.

☑ Volunteer for at least two hours at a pride event or festival.

☑ Join at least one community organization, such as a local choir, Pride planning board, Lesbian Avengers, NOW, festival board, or other club.

❏ Help start another Amazon Girl tribe.

❏ At least four times in the next year, contact your lawmakers or write to your local newspaper about an issue near and dear to your community. This could be gay, ethnic minority or women's issues, child abuse, the environment; you know the drill.

blue

SOCIAL DIRECTOR
(Don't expect gratitude for your efforts)

"Sociopaths need to belong, too."

Since humans have gathered around the hearth fires, there's always been someone in any group who's been the one to say, "I know what let's do! Let's all go to the glaciers and ride the mastodons!" Why, even my mom told us about old George S., whom no girl wanted to date but who always had great ideas for fun things to do. Poor old George didn't have the sense (or the ovaries) to be an Amazon Girl, where such skills are not only valued but also sure to earn you a badge. To earn this badge, perform four of the following:

❑ Calculate the carrying capacity of all the vehicles available to your tribe. Consider space for persons in their varying sizes and agilities as well as cooler chests, picnic baskets, walkers and lawn chairs.

❑ List four group activities that (except for food and fuel) cost participants nothing.

❑ List four other activities that cost under $10 each.

❑ Pretend some hugely rich person has made a grant of say, about $10,000 to your tribe. What activity would you plan?

❑ Allow one other person to plan an entire event without unsolicited suggestions (no, I didn't say "meddling," don't be so sensitive) or criticisms from you. Attend the event. Learn one new thing from it.

❑ List two things you can do to console yourself and maintain the friendships when none of your friends shows up for the event you planned that they all said was such a neat idea.

❑ Suggest a way to ensure attendance at an event that several people have said they'll go to. If it works, share this suggestion with the organizers in your community.

yellow

SPORTS

Not all of us are athletic, but sports do make up a large part of our shared cultures. The non-athletes pretend to be above it all, and the athletes think everyone else is a sissy. Here's your chance to develop some cross-cultural knowledge that might be useful at parties. To earn this badge, perform all of the following:

☑ Attend a live sports event of any kind. It needn't be a professional game. Make a note of any good sportsmanship you observe from participants or observers, and any bad. Consider how it makes each person appear to the world in general. Bring out these observations next time you're around a group that's talking about sports.

❑ Check out a library book dealing with some sport about which you know nothing. Learn what the object of the game/sport is, what its scoring methods are, what skills are needed, and even a bit of its history. Give yourself extra points if you actually understand cricket or curling. Than you can explain it to us.

❑ Take part in a game or athletic contest without causing permanent injury to yourself. If you're unable to find a game to join, go into your back yard and jump rope for five minutes a day for a week. If you're incapacitated, devise a beneficial form of exercise you can perform and do that.

❑ Learn the names of three athletes or sports figures, and try to remember what it is they do.

❑ Learn the names of three sports teams. You may incorporate this in your nature badge by looking their mascots up in a bird book. If the mascot is a bus, never mind.

red

PARTY!

It's important to know how to attend and how to throw a good party. Note: when we say throw, your ex is not the party we have in mind. Remember that the idea of a party is for everyone, host and guest, to have a good time. To earn this badge, perform five of the following:

❑ Read a book on etiquette, paying particular attention to the parts about being a guest and being a host. We recommend Miss Manners because she's sensible and moves with the times.

❑ If your mom didn't make you do this, practice saying "Thank you, Xxx, for inviting me to this lovely/fabulous/exciting party. I had a great time." in front of a mirror.

❑ Think of four ideas for party entertainment, and identify what sorts of partygoers would happily participate in each.

❑ Suggest two ways of encouraging lively conversation and/or interaction among guests who don't know each other well.

❑ Suggest three kinds of food to serve at a party, that you could afford, that most people would enjoy, and they'd wish they had more of.

❑ Decide what your views are on costumes and party décor. Poll at least three of your friends on this issue. This should tell you whether it's a good idea to throw a "come naked" party, or one with funny hats and noisemakers.

❑ Throw a party.

❑ Attend a party; have a good time even if it kills you. Award yourself extra points if you can help someone else have a good time too.

orange

"HERSTORY" AND YOUR PLACE IN IT

The community is divided on whether the word "herstory" is a meaningless abomination of the language, or a reclamation of a part of education hitherto locked away from 50% of the world's population. Either way, trite as this may sound, it's useful to know where we used to be in order to know who we are now. To earn this badge, perform four of the following:

❑ Review five lesbian writings dating back to Sappho. Send your reviews to any publication or organization you think would benefit from them.

❑ Draw a timeline showing at least ten major gay/lesbian/women's events.

❑ Make a scrapbook of your own community's history and donate it to either a local organization or a conservative lawmaker.

❑ Perform an impersonation of a historical or current gay/lesbian/feminist figure.

❑ Explain how we benefit from knowing our history.

❑ Research and report on one historical figure from another culture. Share this new information with your family or your tribe, preferably over dinner.

purple

COMING OUT

To earn this badge, perform all of the following:

❏ Tell three of the following people:

Yourself

Your mom

Your grandmom. Don't be surprised that she already knows.

Your boss.

Your hairdresser.

Your best friend from high school, unless she was your first lover.

Your husband. Aaaargh!

Your oldest child. Fear not, s/he will tell the others.

❏ Display a rainbow flag, pink triangle, or other clearly recognized symbol on your vehicle, home, or office.

❑ Display a picture of your sweetie or, if you have no sweetie, of Xena, on your desk at work and be prepared to explain who she is, in a direct and casual way of course.

Sponsor an acquaintance in her process by doing two of the following, and do not have an affair with her or fix her up with a friend:

❑ Take her to your local bookstore or community center.

❑ Accompany her to a concert, pride event, or potluck.

❑ Lend her a humorous coming-out book or something by Pat Califia, depending on her progress.

❑ Give her web addresses or phone numbers for PFLAG, NGLTF, and at least one major festival.

maple leaf

THE WORLD AROUND YOU

Amazon Girls appreciate the value of having a good healthy planet to live on. They realize that it's just not possible for anyone to live a good life if our only home is polluted, defoliated, covered in concrete, or turned into a giant strip mall.

The more outdoorsy Amazon Girls tend to become dewy-eyed at the prospect of spending extended periods of time in the great outdoors, swatting mosquitoes and trying to build a campfire with wet wood and a depleted Zippo their exes left in the glove compartment. Many mistresses and other sybarites are a bit more restrained in their ecstasy about earth-related activities, but are able to at least understand why it's important to step outdoors and say "Hello" to the birds once in a while.

Even if you'd much rather stay indoors and read a junk novel this weekend, force yourself to try something new. Select one of the badges below and complete a requirement or two. You might learn something. You might have fun. Hell, you might even do some little thing to benefit Mother Earth and won't that be a good feeling, especially when your friends find out and think you did it because you were a good person?

green

NATURE

You know how if you take too much of an antibiotic, or the wrong kind of antibiotic, it kills off the natural flora and fauna in your system and your skin starts itching or you get the runs or you get yeast infections? Probably that's how humanity makes the earth feel. Makes you wonder, doesn't it, how much longer she'll put up with this destructive itchy pest before flushing it out of her system entirely.

However can we put things right? Only one person at a time can, apparently, and then only if that person is willing to make time in her life to learn about, love, and give back to this splendid little planet. Perform three of the following:

- ❏ Plant a tree. Better still, plant a row of them.

- ❏ Donate time (at least twice a year) or money (whatever you can spare, at least once a year) to at least one planet-protecting organization, such as Green Peace, Nature Conservancy, or your local Audubon Society.

- ❏ Research and report to your tribe on a non-human life form, including details about its habitat, feeding, reproductive habits, and what makes it so extraordinary.

- ❏ Be able to identify and tell a bit about at least five native trees.

- ❏ Take a walk at least once a week. Select at least one live thing to notice and observe each time.

blue

THE BEASTS AND THE CHILDREN

Perform at least four of the following:

❑ Be able to identify and tell about five different native vertebrates and five native invertebrates.

❑ Share your critter-knowledge with one or more children, in whatever way you choose. Some ways could be: offer to put up a display at your local public or school library, read books to young children.

❑ Select one non-human living thing to be responsible for, for a year or for the duration of its natural life, whichever is longer. (No fair killing it if you get tired of the project). This could include feeding birds in your yard or apartment, adopting a pet, or caring for a garden bed at a nearby park or other public place.

❑ Make a point to improve conditions for a living thing at least once a month. This could include writing to lawmakers about humane laws or abuse protections, putting up a feeding station for wild animals or birds, volunteering at the local humane organization, or rescuing a bat from a public building before some murderous person smashes it with a broom.

❑ Speak nicely to your sweetie, your child, or your pet at least once a day.

❑ Decorate your home with some artwork that commemorates live things. This could include drawings, photos, collages, a display of seashells, or other creative things.

yellow

THE GARDEN

Gardens are good things. If you don't plow up large areas of native plants to install one, or load yours up with deadly chemicals like pesticides and herbicides, they're good for the environment. If you work in yours regularly, they're good for you. You'll be happy in your garden. If you aren't, seek counseling. To earn this badge, perform either this:

- ❏ Plant a garden. If you live in an apartment, consider container gardening, or locate a city garden project, or offer to help a landed friend with hers. (I accept. You'll find my website address at the back of this book.)

- ❏ Tend your garden, for the entire growing season. Put it to bed for the winter. If you don't have a winter, well, aren't you fortunate?

Or perform all of these:

- ❏ Read an entire book on a garden subject.

❑ Keep a journal about your garden or one you view regularly, for the entire growing season.

❑ Read your journal one winter day when you're home with the flu.

❑ Be able to name at least three garden catalogs you get flooded with in January.

❑ Next year, plant at least one new variety of flower or veggie in your garden or someone else's (you might want to ask permission first).

red

HIKING

If you've never gone camping with your pals, you've missed a treat. By "pals", of course I mean your real pals, your tribe, the ones who know how to enjoy their cholesterol-laden meals and can also stop and admire a blue jay. To earn this badge, take a hike. Who knows? You might like it so much you do it all the time—like once a year. To perform the minimum requirements for this badge, you need only do the following steps one time. (Get it? Steps? Hiking? Har.) To enhance your life, go on outings like this several times a year.

❏ Research some hiking areas that you can reach within a reasonable time—a couple of hour's drive should be the maximum. Parks or recreation areas are a good possibility. Pick up brochures from your local visitor's center, Chamber of Commerce, or call your parks department and have them mail information to you if you can't find something on the web.

❏ Report to your tribe about two of these areas, describing the terrain, things to see and do, cost, accessibility, and other facts that might interest them.

❏ Sit down with your hiking pals and plan a hike. It should be strenuous enough to challenge you but moderate enough that you're able to move the next day without screaming in agony. If you don't have at least one hiking pal, forget about working on this badge until you've done some serious remedial work on your social skills. Trust us on this; if nobody will hike with you, you can bet a hired friend won't throw you a rope if you're stuck in the quicksand. Remember the old joke: "I don't have to outrun the bear, I only have to outrun you!"

❏ Research the area you'll be hiking in. If it's known for deadly vipers, for example, you'll want to learn all you can about deadly vipers beforehand. Ditto flash floods, quicksand, and rabid rednecks.

❑ Equip yourself for this ordeal, uh, outing. You can go to a recreational store and drop a bundle on this, or you can check with friends and relatives about borrowing what you need. The essentials:

> Water bottle: They sell bottles with straps to sling around your neck or waist, a return to the military canteen idea. One clever gal we know freezes water in her plastic bottle and puts it into her backpack on the side closest to her. Keeps her cool and gives her ice water for some hours. The good news is that if your water bottle feels too heavy, that's an incentive to keep drinking from it.

> Footwear: This should be your own unless you have a friend with uncannily similar feet. Remember fifth-grade health class? That business about comfortable, supportive shoes? They were right.

> Thick absorbent socks are nifty too.

> Comfy clothes, appropriate for the season, are a must. Wear layers; you'll be glad you did.

> Sun block.

> Bug repellent if needed.

Optional but very helpful:

> Backpack to carry all your junk in.

> A lightweight but strong walking stick. Trekking poles are grand if you can borrow one or find it on sale.

> A compass. It may not help you find your way but it looks neat hanging from your pack.

> One of those gadgets that lets you pee standing up. Be sure to practice in the shower before setting out, or you might as well hunker down in the bushes like everyone else and get pee in your shoe that way.

> Do NOT take along a cell phone. You are not eligible for this badge if you do. (Sigh). Yes, you may have one in your car for emergency calls.

❏ This is an important step; plan your menu. Will you have a picnic before or after the hike, or take munchies along on the trail, or both? If you take trail munchies, load them into your pack and walk around your house wearing the pack for a few minutes. If at this point your neck and shoulders are shrieking with pain, you might want to eat your lunch at a nice picnic table before setting out on the trip and just take an apple along for the trail.

❑ Map out your route or trail. Plan to follow existing, marked trails. If you want to do pathfinder activities, be sure to take (and pass) an orienteering class before inflicting such an activity on your tribe. Tell yourself, "It's no disgrace to turn around and go back the way we came in. It's damned embarrassing to have to be rescued by a bunch of young guys."

❑ If you have never hiked before, be sure to take some practice walks in your neighborhood for a week or two in advance. When you can easily walk for half the distance of your planned hike, you just might survive this ordeal.

❑ Go there, do it.

Have fun, but also:

❑ Pay attention to your surroundings.

❑ Identify three things along the trail that could help you find your way.

❑ Identify any five flowers, birds or trees along the way.

❑ Notice how the clouds look, and the color of the sky at various times.

❑ Report on your hike to your tribe. Describe how you celebrated or relaxed at the end of the trail.

orange

CAMPING

This is is like the hiking badge, except you actually camp out to earn this. Read the hiking badge requirements for helpful hints, and also do the following:

❑ Sit down with your pals and plan your campout. For your first adventure, you should probably limit the time to one or two nights. This way you have a likelihood of ending up speaking to one another at the end of the time.

❑ Do the same research about the campground that you would for a hike, but really, really concentrate on the safety issue; state or national park campgrounds are patrolled regularly and you stand a better chance of coming home alive from those. If you can find a women-only location beside a festival, tell us about it so we can go too.

❑ Equip yourself. The essentials:

Food: If you have your picnicking badge, you know what to do. If you don't, go look at the requirements. Be sure to coordinate with your pals so you don't end up with six bottles of olive oil and no vinegar.

Remember that food will need to be stored for 1-2 days, so spoilable food needs to live in your cooler with plenty of ice. Most campgrounds have camp stores where you can get more ice.

Clothing: You know how to dress comfortably, you're lesbians, for crying out loud. Plan for it to be colder and hotter than you expect, and maybe it will rain, too.

Shelter: Some tough folks sleep out under the stars. Unless you have a good climate, lots of privacy, no phobias and no ticks, mosquitoes, etc, you'll probably want to borrow a tent. Practice putting it up in your back yard first, you'll be glad you did. This will help you identify how many pieces are missing and devise a substitute, thus achieving one of the requirements for the Building and Tool Usage badge.

Sleeping bags are not essential—you can bring along your favorite blankie and pillow, but you'll probably want a pad or air mattress under your aging, aching bones.

Money; You'll need some cash for campground fees and ice and getting an ice-cream cone, but don't bring a big wad of valuable stuff.

Gadgets: Most campgrounds have picnic tables and fire pits. You'll need to bring all your cooking utensils that fit your menu, and cleaning supplies for them. You'll want something to haul water in. Go through the activities of daily living in your mind and plan what you'll need to carry them out when you're not in your own kitchen, shower, pantry, etc.

See hiking equipment for helpful outdoorsy stuff.

❑ Report on your campout to your tribe. Tell them about one thing you forgot to bring and how you managed without it. Tell them about one great thing that happened that you didn't expect.

purple

OUTDOOR ACTIVITIES

Our moms were right. (About some things, anyway). It's a lot healthier and happier for us to drag our lazy butts up off the couch and go outside and play. Ever since we quit doing that, let's face it, our lives have been lackluster and depressing. "Speak For yourself," you say? Then why are you seeing that dental surgeon about your abruxia, that chiropractor for neck spasms, that therapist for general angst, and popping Prozac in between times? Don't argue with your mom, go outside and play.

❑ Obtain one of the following items of inexpensive equipment:
A beach badminton set.

A kite rated "easy to fly" and 500 feet of string for it.

A fishing pole with line, sinker, and bobber, and a container of bait.

A net bag to collect neat stuff in

A bottle of bubble soap and bubble-blowing pipe.
Softball and mitt.

❑ Put on a pair of really comfortable shoes that can get dirty, and put a trashy novel in your pocket for rest periods.

❑ Pack a lunch including any of the following. Do not include wine, paté, or anything labeled "organic" or, worse yet, "lite":
    Peanut butter sandwich with jelly or mayo
    Banana or apple
    Cookies
    Small container of juice
    The kind of candy bar you used to love as a kid
    Chips, no salsa
    Carrot slices
    Velveeta cheese

❑ Put on your comfortable shoes, comfy clothes, and rain or snow gear as needed. Tell someone where you're going—or persuade her to come with you.

❏ Open the door. Step outside. Close the door, flies will get in, where were you raised, in a barn? Spend a moment analyzing current atmospheric conditions. That bright stuff coming from the sky is called "sunshine." The wet stuff is "rain." If it's really cold wet stuff, it might be "snow." Be able to identify these.

❏ Go to where you can use your equipment. If you can walk there, give yourself extra points.

❏ Sit on the riverbank and fish. Or fly your kite. Or blow bubbles. Or play catch or badminton with your companion. Kick up dirt with your shoes.

❏ Eat your sandwich. (If you've been fishing, wipe your hands off first). Read some of your trashy novel.

❏ Pick up a pretty stone to give to someone you love.

❏ Do this again on Saturday.

oak leaf

LIVING WELL

Since my sweetie and I began to live together, we've fallen into patterns and ways of living that suit us both. Some things we brought with us, others we've devised together, usually by one of us saying with the brashness of a five-year-old, "I know what let's do!" followed by the other's saying "Nah, we can't do that," followed by both of us saying, "Why not?" Sometimes we've ended up peering out of the rubble, saying "Oh. That's why not. Next time we'll call the plumber first," but oftener the result is some really neat way of doing things, and so we keep it. Life is an adventure when an Amazon Girl approaches things this way. Sometimes you could end up in the snake pit; sometimes you could achieve your Goddess rank. At least you'll never be bored.

We observe, sometimes with sad bemusement, that some couples' patterns and habits suit only one of the pair, and sometimes suit neither, yet these people stick grimly to the familiar, if unpleasant, routines long after any sensible primate would have given up and done something more fun, like becoming Alpha leader by dint of banging gasoline cans together. These unfortunate folks do stuff they saw their parents do, or stuff they see on TV that seems like it ought to be neat, or, I dunno, stuff they think rich people do and so it must be classy.

You have no doubt overheard other people envying rock stars, football players and lottery winners, even though those people are clearly not living happy lives, in their attack-dog patrolled mansions, by any standards. One sensible Tomboy once said, "What good is a house with all those rooms? How many rooms do you spend most of your time in anyway? All you'd have is more space to keep clean!"

The guidelines below give you a good start on the fine art of Living Well. You may fine-tune your skills by earning the various badges under this heading. Then you can write your own guidelines and annoy all your tribe members by sharing them whenever an opportunity comes up.

1) NO television. Life's short, why waste it on electronic crap that's designed to sell you stuff you never wanted or needed in the first place? In your spare time, read a book. Talk to your sweetie. Take a class. Or take a walk. Not in a shopping mall. Watch a nature video, and learn about the hot and slippery sex lives of banana slugs. Tell your tribe about it, but not during dinner.

2) Choose friends wisely. Amazon Girls have a few good friends; they're called "a tribe." We love them, and they seem to love us. Or at least they keep their nausea under control when we're around them.

3) Live on the planet you have. This means, keep in touch with your real neighbors: the blue jay family in the tree out back, the tiny but determined spider who makes her web in the corner of the garage, the tulip which was misplaced by that damned squirrel, the maple which has sex with itself every year and drops seeds all over your yard. Hey, just because plants live slower lives than ours doesn't mean they don't have rich, active lives.

4) Live in the home you have. Large or small, tidy or un-, it's your space. Take charge of it, instead of vice-versa. Fill it with books and music, photos you've taken yourself, and plants. Light candles. Burn some incense. If you find you're collecting too much clutter, maybe it's a sign that you feel empty somewhere else. Give some things away. Feed the birds.

5) Exercise: Skip it. Have you ever seen a happy jogger? (Just kidding).

6) Plant your garden, and tend it. Admire it on good days. It will give you fresh air, herbs and

flowers, and great food for conversation. Live in an apartment? What's the matter, you never heard of pots?

7) Food: your body is a temple. Bad analogy—temples don't need to be fed, but we do.

The idea that many people come home and pop a cardboard tray into the microwave each evening fills us with pity. Unless we are forced by circumstances or civic responsibility to go out, each evening we well-adjusted Amazon Girls sit down together at the dinner table and enjoy real food, which one or the other of us has lovingly cooked. You must cook lovingly if you're going to cook. In fact, even if you don't cook, do it lovingly. Linger over the heating of that can of Campbell's Chicken Noodle! Stir it sensually with a wooden spoon! Add some cinnamon to that Instant Oatmeal! You can do it!

But really, there's just no sense in eating if you aren't going to have real food. (Secret: real food costs less than the artificial kind.) And there's no sense in having real food unless you put a clean cloth on the table, use dishes you like, put your beverage of choice into nice glasses (unless you threw them all at your ex and can't afford new ones just yet). Beverage of choice? Sparkling water, maybe, or cranberry juice. Wine, if you like it, or cider. PLEASE please please, eschew diet drinks. If you must poison your system with strangely processed chemicals, you might as well stir some garden fertilizer into laundry detergent and drink that. Honestly.

To make your new regimen complete, here (gratis) are two nice things to have at your next tribal potluck:

HARRIET'S WONDERFUL SALAD
Ingredients:

Greens and lettuces: Endive, radicchio, spinach, Boston, Bibb, or other assorted leaf lettuces and greens, washed, drained, and torn lightly. Do NOT use that tasteless nasty iceberg lettuce unless you're under siege and you've used all the dandelions in your yard and you can't find anything else at all.

Carrots, peppers, radishes, tomatoes, washed and cut into chunks to suit your taste.

Olive oil.

Vinegar: wine, tarragon or balsamic, anything but white vinegar, which is good for removing hard water scale from your pots.

Basil, garlic, oregano, pepper, dill. Any of these, or add your favorite.

Optional: palm hearts, artichoke hearts, avocado, boiled egg pieces, olives, green onion slices, be creative here.

Stir 2 tbs. oil and a splash of vinegar into salad bowl; stir in herbs. Add lettuce and other veggies, toss lightly (clean hands work best for this, or use two forks).

Serve with the meal, but be really brave and try eating the salad after your entree.

JEWISH MOM'S CHICKEN SOUP
Ingredients:
1 whole chicken.
2 onions.
Several small carrots, or 3 large carrots cut into 1-inch chunks.
1 medium-sized parsnip, cut into chunks.
Dill weed.
Salt.
Optional: Rice or Farfel.

Remove innards and large fat deposits from chicken, rinse bird. Place in large pot, cover with cold water, and boil, skimming off foam as it appears. After half an hour, turn heat back to simmer; add onions, carrots, parsnip, dill. Salt to taste. Simmer for 1 hour. Remove bird and allow to cool before removing meat from the bones and returning to pot. Add rice or farfel; simmer for 15–30 more minutes.

Serve as a meal with salad and bread, or for medicinal purposes, have a small bowl of this before your regular dinner.

green

PICNICKING

A picnic is a meal served in an unusual location, usually outdoors. Of course you can picnic in your living room, or even better, in your bed. The important thing is to gather up your meal and move it somewhere else. To earn this badge, you must have a picnic with a pal or a sweetie. If the pal and the sweetie are one and the same, why, aren't you fortunate? On second thought, have a second picnic too. No, you don't get a badge for each picnic; don't be greedy. Share your cookies.

If you don't have some clever ideas about picnic fare and settings, feel free to plagiarize. Give yourself extra points if you can work in candles, small container of flowers, or cloth napkins. Here are picnics we've been on or heard about:

- ❏ Go to the deli of your local grocery and get a roasted chicken and some Chinese slaw. Spread a blanket under the tree in your back yard on a sunny Memorial Day weekend. Open a bottle of white wine to go with your chicken.

- ❏ Make peanut butter sandwiches, place in a brown paper bag with carrot sticks, cookies, apples, and a bottle of fruit juice. Walk down a country road until you find a pasture that's not posted "No trespassing." Spread your jackets on the ground to sit on while you eat your lunches. Note to city A.G.s: Those brown squishy things come from a part of the cow you only eat in hot dogs. Don't sit on them.

- ❏ Load up your cooler chest with hot dogs, condiments, cheese sticks, marshmallows, and other unhealthy things. Bring along some charcoal and lighter stuff, and some cooking forks or wire coat hangers. Go to a local park. Fire up the charcoal in a grill, play Frisbee until the coals are ready, cook the hotdogs and marshmallows.

- ❏ Do the same as above, but bring steaks and potatoes to bake in the coals. You can roast corn on the cob in coals too, just leave the husks on and soak the ears in clean water so they steam rather than scorch. If you're a vegan, skip the steak, just open your canister of lentils and look virtuous rather than wistful as you eat them.

❑ On a rainy day (or night), put cheese, fruit, juice, crusty bread, and chocolate on a tray. Bring tray to bedroom, where your sweetie is just waking up or just getting into bed. Feed each other.

❑ Pretend to be heterosexuals. Go to a fast-food chain. Purchase a Big Mac, fries, and diet coke. Carry your tray of food into the crowded "dining" area. Eat your meal, snapping and snarling at each other as you do so. Take an antacid tablet for dessert. Get into your car and drive home too fast, bitching about the traffic.

❑ Arrange to meet your tribe at a park or someone's back yard. It's best if the yard belongs to someone you know, but who are we to stifle your sense of adventure? Everyone bring her own meal. Sit in a circle and pass food around. Extra points here if you sample something new.

blue

SPIRITUALITY

This is where you get to think about your personal place in the universe. To earn this badge, perform all of the following:

❑ Research three world religions or belief systems. Mention two benefits and two drawbacks to each of these.

❑ Think about your own belief system in terms of:

How the universe began.

What keeps it running.

Our planet's place in it.

Our species; its ideal vs. actual place in the universe.

❑ Think of a way to exemplify your belief system in your everyday life. If you can do this without ostentatious displays or speechmaking, so much the better.

❑ Allow a few minutes for yourself each day to "center" or renew yourself. If your life is too busy for this, then write a brief essay about what you think the purpose of your life is.

❑ Select one small, unobtrusive life form to cherish and nurture. This may be a weed in your garden, a spider in the corner of your kitchen, or a particular bird at your feeder. Regularly spend a few moments contemplating this being for the duration of its brief life. No fair killing it if you get tired of this exercise.

❑ Discover the rudiments of someone else's belief system. Try not to be judgmental about anything you disagree with, but consider why they believe as they do and what they gain from those beliefs. Do you gain the same benefits from your beliefs? Why or why not?

yellow

MAKING A FASHION STATEMENT

"I had such a bad hair day that I looked like a rooster. Now I just call it my cock-a-doodle-do." To earn this badge, perform all of the following:

❑ Clean out your closet. Get rid of stuff:

That no longer fits you.

That fits but it's ugly so you never wear it.

That's so ratty and/or stained you feel creepy when you wear it.

That's beige. Author's note: By this, of course we mean anything you wear on your self-effacing days. Don't give us a hard time about this one.

If you're a round person, ditch those vertical stripes. That's a myth perpetuated by people who don't like round people.

❑ Pick up a copy of any fashion magazine from your local newsstand. Read it, paying particular attention to the ads, which will probably be most of it. Snicker. Throw it away.

❑ Save your allowance and purchase an item of clothing that makes you feel good when you wear it.

❑ Devise one emergency "fix" for a bad hair day. Suggest it to your friends.

❑ Practice responding gracefully to compliments: "Why, thank you," "How kind of you to say so." Mistresses, practice saying, "How clever of you to notice."

❑ When you're out in a crowd, pretend you're a slinky black cat with large green eyes.

❑ Warriors: If you have a sweetie, find out what outfits or type of outfits she likes you to wear. Wear these.

❑ Mistresses: If you have a sweetie or admirer, find out what outfits or type of outfits she likes you to wear. Wear whatever you feel sexy in; she'll just have to cope.

VACATIONING

Taking a good vacation is an art, but even so you can certainly learn the basics. To earn this badge, do all of the following:

❑ Identify at least four really cool spots to spend your vacation in. Describe their good points.

❑ Select one of those spots and plan your trip there, considering transportation, accommodations, meals, cost, traveling companions.

❑ Go there, virtually if not in fact. Assemble a small scrapbook or photo album with captions telling how it went.

❑ Plan and go on at least two mini-trips that involve staying over at least one night. Tell about the accommodations, sights along the way, meals and why or why not you'd like to repeat this trip.

❑ Identify these styles of luggage and describe who'd be most likely to carry them:

Matched Kroger

Assorted unmatched hard-sided bags from parents' attic and last two breakups

Rolling suitcase with collapsing handle

Nylon zipper carry bags

Backpack and pockets.

❑ Demonstrate the best way to pack your own stuff in one of these.

TO YOUR VERY GOOD HEALTH

"Tyrone, you know how much I enjoy watching you work. But I have a wedding to plan, a wife to murder, and Guilder to frame for it."

"Get some rest. If you haven't got your health, you haven't got anything."

—The Princess Bride

To earn this badge, and ensure your future well being, perform both of the following:

❑ If you haven't already done so this year, make an appointment with your local doctor or clinic for a checkup. Go to it. Pay attention to your doctor's suggestions. If you disagree with any, be sure you have better reasons for this than "I don't wanna hear it."

For the next two months:

- ❏ Walk or otherwise be active for at least 20 minutes a day, four days a week.

- ❏ Spend at least 10 minutes a day doing nothing. Try to think of pleasant things at that time.

- ❏ Drink water or fruit or veggie juices during the day rather than pop, coffee or diet concoctions.

- ❏ Eat at least one piece of fresh fruit a day.

- ❏ If you are a smoker, make a serious effort to reduce your tobacco intake by half, by the end of the period. Bonus points if you can quit entirely.

- ❏ If you are a regular user of controlled substances, ditto the above.

- ❏ If you are a heavy drinker of alcohol (more than two drinks a day), join AA.

- ❏ Take a class or read a book about something you've never been interested in before.

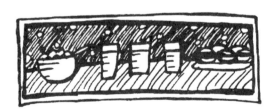

purple

ARTS & MUSIC

A rt needn't be snobbish and wimpy. Earn this badge with gusto, by performing two from each section of the following:

ARTS

❑ Purchase or check out from the library two books about art. Read these and try to understand the concepts. You don't need to read all the footnotes.

❑ Visit an art museum or gallery. Pay attention.

❑ Learn the primary and secondary colors, and tell which are complementary.

❑ Create a work of art. Show it to at least two people.

MUSIC

❑ Purchase or check out from the library two recordings of music of a type you don't normally listen to. Listen to them with full attention; try to understand, if not appreciate, this style of music.

❑ Attend a live concert, your choice. Note that it's usually possible to find cheap or free concerts, if only by attending some church that has a music program, or a children's performance in a local school. Check your local newspaper under the public calendar section.

❑ Learn to play or hum or whistle the C major scale.

❑ Sing a song in front of at least two people.

pink

READING

Yes, we know you know how to read, or why would you be looking at this book? Unless, of course, you're really invested in faking it, in which case thanks for choosing this book for your display of literacy. Except that would mean you can't read this anyway, so why am I bothering to thank you? Get someone else to read you this part so you can be thanked.

We digress (ahem). Too many of us say things like "I'm just so busy I don't have time to read these days". To which we Amazon Girls say, "bushwah", "oh, bosh", or "bullshit", depending on our orientation. If you have time to go to the bathroom, or drink a morning cup of coffee, or sit on the couch in front of the Plug-In Drug (aka television), you have time to pick up a book and read a page or two. Or even earn this badge, by doing all of the following:

❑ If you don't already have one, go to your nearest public library and obtain a library card. Put this into your wallet near your check-cashing card so you can find it easily.

❑ Read ten books that you have not read before. At least one of these books should be about a subject you are not familiar with, and another should be of a sort you don't usually read. For example, if you normally read novels, get a collection of essays. Yes, you could cheat and page through ten short kids' books. No, you will not have gained anything by doing that, and you'll feel silly doing the next requirements.

❑ Select one of those ten books and tell your tribe about it. If you can inspire at least one tribe member to read that book for herself, award yourself extra points.

❑ Select another one of those ten books and learn something about its author. If the author is still living and you really loved the book, write to her/him and tell her/him so.

❑ Select another of those ten books and learn more about its subject, or the book's setting, or any historical character mentioned in it.

Do one of the following:

❑ Check out at least one book from the kids' section of the library. Don't be embarrassed by this, lots of grownups check out kid books for nieces and nephews; the librarians think nothing of it. Find a child to read this book to. You might want to practice reading aloud from this book first. No kidding, you'd be amazed at what you could find yourself stuck in, trying to read aloud from a book with lots of sound effects or critter noises, if you don't practice it.

❑ Join a reading discussion group and stick with it for at least two months.

❑ Go to a nursing home and read aloud (poetry, essays or short stories are the best for this) to someone whose eyesight is gone. Be sure you contact the person at the front desk and make arrangements ahead of time.

❑ Throw a party where guests take turns reading aloud a favorite short story or poem, or where the group does a dramatic reading of a short play, each person taking a different character.

AMAZON GIRLS IN ACTION

WHERE DO WE BEGIN? AND OTHER FREQUENTLY ASKED QUESTIONS.

S ince its inception , Amazon Girls has heard from many interested women and a few interested men, and their questions have generally boiled down to these:

Q: How do I join?
A: You gather your pals together and form a tribe. Take charge of your destinies! Your tribe can be whatever you decide to make of it.

(Brief rant begins here, and you're perfectly welcome to skip it and move on to the next question):

There is an unfortunate tendency among Homo sapiens to want someone else to arrange a women's center/party/organization/potluck/government/workshop/independent bookstore, so the rest of us can patronize it at our leisure and criticize the creator and tell how we would have done it.

We, the Amazon Girl founders, have no interest in doing all this for you. You're big kids, we assume, and know as well as anybody how to pick up the telephone or log on and invite some friends over to chat about forming a tribe.

This is not something to lose sleep over; it's just a fun way to organize your activities and interests. Dip into the handbook; work on some badges if you like, or if you'd rather, you can sit around drinking tea and discussing how you'd have done it better if you were founding an organization.

You DON'T need to wear dorkey uniforms. You don't need to pay dues, drink Kool-Aid, meet regularly, or any of those "official" things, unless, of course, that's what your tribe gets into. Just please, whatever you all decide to do with your tribe, do it with gusto. Pretend you're living in a beer commercial.

(End of Rant. More questions follow.)

Q: I have no pals because,
    1. I'm new to town
    2. I've just come out
    3. I have absolutely no social skills and everyone runs away the second they lay eyes on me
    4. I live out in the country and the only other lesbians nearby are this crabby old pair of closeted bulldykes who own the local greasy spoon and refuse to look at me.
    How do I form a tribe by myself?

A: 1. This is a great way to meet people. Make a flyer (see insert) announcing the formation of a new tribe and hang it in your local womens' center/bookstore/womens' bar/sex toy store/UU church. Be sure to include your contact information. Make it look cute and perky, and before you know it you'll have lots of pals.

2. This is scarier. Work on your Coming Out badge before even thinking of doing anything else, and then you'll be in better shape to do Step 1, above.

3. Read *Miss Manners*, and then as your act of moral will, practice, practice, practice controlling those unpleasant impulses of yours to do things like score points against those around you, assholean as they may truly be. At the end of your Tomboy period, Amazon Girls hope you will have acquired some pals who will want to go to the playground with you.

4. This is harder, and all you can do is form long-distance friendships. Consider forming an E-tribe, using chat rooms and listservs to stay in touch with your tribe.

Q: There's a group of us that gets together twice a year to camp out and party. Could we be an Amazon Girl tribe?

A: Sounds to us like you already are. At your next gathering, make plans for a stomping-up ceremony to be held at the following gathering. S'mores and a fish fry, yum!

SAMPLE FLYER/SIGN-UP SHEET

JOIN THE AMAZON GIRLS TODAY!

Amazon Girls is a community of out, proud lesbians who seek adventure, whimsy and the rekindling of ancient dreams. We're forming a tribe right here in our own city. Come to the meeting and find out all about it!

Date/Time:	Tuesday, March 28, 2003
Location:	Wilhelmina and Josephine Clarissa's
Agenda:	Orientation, food, gossip
	Decide on outfits
	Decide on tribal name

Or,

Amazon Girls is a community of out, proud lesbians who seek adventure, whimsy and the rekindling of ancient dreams. We're forming a tribe right here in our own city. Give us your name, email address and/or phone number and we'll be contacting you:

_____

_____

_____

_____

AMAZON GIRLS ON THE ROAD

The first-ever Amazon Girl tribe, the Trailblazers, wasn't really the first tribe at all. No, we realized that we had been Amazon Girls for many years without realizing it, and the tribe varied only slightly by name and make-up. In every case, there were two or more pals in search of adventure, fun, ways to cope with a hostile society, or ways to learn and grow. Here are histories of some of our tribes; if you substitute 'tribe' for 'softball team', 'campers' or 'chorus', you'll have the idea.

"THE TRIBE" PLAYS SOFTBALL

In the summer of 1987, several gym-class dropouts gathered together and formed the TLC Draggins, a completely new concept in softball teams. The Draggins were based on the bizarre notion that softball is a recreational game and therefore should be fun and entertaining rather than an exercise in pain and humiliation. Most Draggin team members had a history of childhood gym-class abuse and torture. Our ineptness, myopsy, fatness and shortness of breath separated us from our jock sisters and made us objects of ridicule, usually in the eyes of the very women we desperately longed to impress. As adults, we still harbored a longing to play the game, to belong to a team with neat uniforms, to be heroes.

The Draggins accepted anyone who wanted to show up one evening a week, purchase and wear a team shirt, follow the rules, and eat pizza. Requirements were few, but some rules were unbending:

1. If it hurts, don't do it. There's no sense in injuring yourself just to catch a fabric-covered sphere* before someone else arrives at a purposeless destination. Still, all players are expected to participate enthusiastically while observing safety recommendations.

2. Absolutely no abuse or ridicule of team members is allowed. Self-abuse and abuse of onlookers is optional.

3. Players can be on whichever team they choose (details later); the childhood torture ritual of "choosing up sides" is not allowed.

4. Gloating over final scores is frowned upon, to such an extent that the team quickly modified the rules to set the score back to 0 at the start of each inning.

* Fabric-covered? FABRIC-COVERED? Well, yes. Draggins quickly learned that if they didn't duck quickly enough, any hit ball could really hurt. One Draggin broke a finger trying to catch a fast-moving softball. Fortunately, Babe discovered a padded, fabric-covered ball which performed as well for Draggin purposes and hurt much less on impact.

Draggins quickly learned the secret thrill of being able to say casually, "No, not Thursday, I have softball that night" to acquaintances. They learned the joys of showing up at the pizza place in their cool shirts, sweaty leather glove hanging casually from one finger, reserving a large table for "the rest of the team." When asked by onlookers, "Who won?", they could always say "We did!", mainly because the Draggins have never, in their five-year history, played against anyone but themselves.

"So how," you may ask, "did you get two teams?" Easy. When Draggins first signed up for the team, the organizer would ask them for their shirt size, desired team name, of which more later, and "What number do you want on the back? We have 7 and 13 left." When the team gathered on the first evening, therefore, there were only 7s and 13s, thus providing a good random mix of players for two teams, and usually ensuring that couples were separated by team. This latter condition ensured that most players had someone to hug them when they arrived at Second and also to lend sincerity to the cheers for the other side.

Team names? Players were told to come up with a nickname, the kind of thing they'd dreamed, in secret fantasies, that kids had called them when they were twelve. Names like "Slim," "Swifty," and "Slugger," a name to conjure great memories with. Nonetheless, several wags came up with names like "Old Bat" and "Balls," "Smut" and "Wuss." Names were only limited by what would fit across the back of a shirt, and since several XXL folks were on the team, that wasn't much of a problem.

"Oh sure," people have said when told of the Draggins, "I once joined a league that claimed to be non-competitive, and a week later it was overrun by jocks. They yelled at me every time I missed the ball and I quit before the season ended." Consider Draggin history, dear reader:

Fuzzy, who played First Base, was not the world's greatest hitter. Consequently, when she finally hit a grounder and ran for First, both teams cheered. She stood proudly on first and watched her teammate get a hit, stood with one foot on First, then called to the other team's shortstop, "Throw it here!"

By the third week, two of the more creative members of this organization were seen carrying their lawn chairs with them to the outfield.

Debbil, one of the few actually talented players, was told, on the second week, "If you hit it past that tree again you'll have to go and bring it back yourself."

One of the more popular Draggin cheers was, "Good A.C.! (almost-catch)." Second favorite was "*You* go bring it back, my feet hurt!"

Bubba, the team captain, won that honored position by showing up for all practices, including one that was canceled.

Eventually, the novelty of the thing wore off. In the fifth summer, attendance dropped off to the point that players had to take turns being hitter and catcher in the same inning. While this is a good exercise in adaptation, it doesn't make for very exciting games. It's been many years since the Draggins convened, but some of us miss those good old days. A lot of friendships formed and ended as a result of this team. Some of us still have our shirts. Maybe one day we'll announce new membership sign-up at a pitch-in, order some more shirts, and scout around for a new pizza place with a park nearby. One without too many trees, and a convenient parking lot.

"THE TRIBE" GOES CAMPING

My sweetie and I love to go camping. We tell anyone who asks that we love it. We love it so much, in fact, that our tribe, in desperate yearning to earn a badge, went camp-ing this weekend for the first time in four years. I'd forgot-ten just how much fun it is. Ah, the fresh air, starry starry nights, singing around the campfire with old friends.

Part I—The Event

For any of you who haven't had this experience, camping is an event wherein people who don't like crowds, grocery shopping, cooking, cleaning, or washing dishes will spend hours shopping for just the right cookout food, charcoal, ice, and drinks and driving for over an hour to a campground packed with good ol' boys who play loud music, drink too much beer, and slap their kids around until all hours of the night.

Amazon Girls will cheerfully assemble a temporary abode from fiberglass rods and nylon, which requires they remove their shoes before entering (more on this later) or immediately sweep the floor if they forget. They'll prepare elaborate meals using primitive utensils (having forgotten to bring most of the useful ones) and sit at a birdshit-covered picnic table eating with a three-tined fork in one hand and waving vainly at flies, yellow jackets and mosquitoes with the other. Afterward they'll expend ten times the effort they'd expend at home trying to clean the dishes by hauling jugs of water from the public well and heating it on a faulty cook stove, not nearly as efficiently as their peasant foremothers did.

After not having slept for two nights because of the raucous neighbors, odd animal sounds at 3:00 am, long hikes to a smelly public toilet, and manic raccoons who drop in several times each night for a little snack, Amazon Girls will literally fold their tents, pack up all their junk, uh, gear, and drag their exhausted bodies home to spend several hours cleaning and putting away said gear. They'll sleep like zombies that night and brag at work the next day about how relaxed and rested they are from their weekend at Shady Acres State Park.

Part II—The Junk, Uh, Gear

Amazon Girl campers come in three general types, the Half-Assed, the Nifty Gadgeteers, and the hybrids. The first view camping as a getaway weekend, and I suspect them of having a sizeable streak of good-ol'-boyism. They toss an old frying pan, some paper plates, a toothbrush and a Frisbee into a grocery bag, borrow a perfectly-folded tent from a Nifty Gadgeteer, and stop somewhere on the way to the campground to pick up a six-pack of something and some potato chips. At the end of the weekend they throw away everything that won't clean easily, spray the inside of the borrowed tent with mildew spores, and drop it on the doorstep of the apoplectic Gadgeteer on their way home. I wish I could be more like them, but find that having a mom who majored in Home Ec. has scarred me deeply.

The Nifty Gadgeteers keep LL Bean and Galyan's in business. They have one or more tents for different uses and kits which nest, screw, snap and Velcro together, holding first aid stuff, cooking stuff, tent-patching stuff, tiny whiskbroom-with-matching-dustpan things, and lanyards, which they know what to do with. They load their gear into their four-wheel-drive camping vehicles in a particular order. They put their ground cloth, which is made from plastic nowadays, in last, so it will be on top when they get to the campsite, since they need it first when they get there. Spare bottle of propane, here. Cooler chest with little matching ice bottles, so. Small unbreakable camper-style rosebud vase, with the tablecloth-and-stainless-steel-napkin-rings kit, thus. You get the picture. I wish I could be more like them, but find that rebelling against a mom who majored in Home Ec. has scarred me deeply.

The hybrids? You probably have guessed it, yes, we are the ones who can't quite bear to live like barbarians even for a weekend, but could never be organized (or wealthy) enough to buy, assemble, pack and remember everything necessary for gracious outdoor living. We buy a nifty kit of some kind from REI Co-op just because the stainless steel napkin rings are so cunning, but then we stuff it into the buffet and can never find it, so at the campsite we slop a bucket of Clorox water over the birdshit-covered table and say it's clean enough to eat from. When we pack to go home, we stand on said table and shake most of the dirt off the ground cloth and out of the tent, and we're sure to start at least one load of laundry before falling into bed when we get home.

I do possess a piece of gear which is the envy of every camper I've met, and that's a canoe which once belonged to the Latta sisters, was bought by my father, hung for a while on Uncle Francis's shed wall, and was rescued by my ex-sweetie and me. We brought it home, cleaned it up, painted it in rainbow colors and named it, in press-on letters, Rainbow Connection. When I was twelve I dreamed of becoming a pirate captain. I love this vintage craft.

My current sweetie is quite aquatic, but she also is short, round, and loses her balance easily. Launching a canoe with her in it would strain the patience and ingenuity of most people; fortunately we're still madly in love and manage the thing with a certain clumsy aplomb.

Part III—Camping With Your Tribe

My sweetie and I planned this recent trip with some dear old friends some time ago. "It's been ages," we agreed, "and this time we're not going to put it off any longer. No excuses, we're going." On the Monday before the trip, two other dear old friends agreed to join us there. On Thursday, the first two DOF's pooped out on us. We announced to each other that they've done this too often lately, and we'll require them to crawl on their bellies like reptiles before we agree to do anything with them ever again. We announce this to each other a lot. We keep arranging outings with them. Latent S/M, I suppose.

We used to have large groups of DOFs meet for camping weekends, but cross-cultural (see Part II) camping proved too stressful for many in the group, especially my previous sweetie. Betsy, we'll call her, is the archetypal Nifty Gadgeteer, and once her campsite is assembled to her satisfaction it's a wonder to behold, the apothecary kit hanging from its proper ring, the easy-to-clean rollup table standing in its proper place. (Yes, there really is such a table, and yes, it's really a nifty thing. No, I never figured out the science of determining its proper place.)

On one of our group trips, one of the novice campers asked to see inside Betsy's tent. "Yes," said Betsy, "but be sure to take your shoes off before you enter." Nonplussed but agreeable, the novice sat down at the picnic table and removed her shoes, then walked across the clearing in her stocking feet, accumulating more dirt, pine needles, and crud on her socks than she ever could have on her shoes, and tracked it all into the tent.

Occurrences like this began to fray Betsy's nerves and temper, and probably one of the major consolations (I'm sure there are many) for her having lost my exquisite companionship is the fact that she no longer has to endure these group agonies in the company of a Hybrid camper.

But I digress. The recent trip involved only two DOF's, now Tomboys, who went to the campground a day before us and secured a lovely site, shaded and right on the bank of a large pond, adjacent to several recreational vehicles full of beer-guzzling, music-playing, kid-smacking troglodytes, and were positively fuming by the time we arrived. One Tomboy, whom we'll call Bubba (long story, never mind), tried to drown them out with her own radio but soon gave up.

We had a lovely breakfast at noon, which resulted in the discovery of two of the First Annual Dyke Camping Olympic Games, of which more later. We realized long ago that the jolliest thing about camping is the meals. Each individual or couple brings her own food and cooking equipment. Five minutes after cooking begins, that Lesbian Food thing kicks in: "We have extra potatoes; should we bake you some also?" "Oh sure, and we've made too much salad so you should have some." "I brought us all cookies to go with Nancy's watermelon for dessert." "Lookie here, wine in a milk carton!" We eat like pigs on these weekends and convince ourselves it's healthy because we've cooked it outdoors (brushing the flies off the grapes when we think of it).

At night we sit around a smoky, too-hot fire and talk about everyone who hasn't come along on the trip. Invariably some idiot wants to have a cozy Group Sing, and everyone except me is very enthusiastic, and everyone except me doesn't know the words. I know all the words, and I'm not telling. I wish they'd stop plaintively asking "Where have all the flowers gone?" and tell me what *really* happened to crazy old Sharon what's-her-name.

Part IV—Tribal Camping Olympic Games

Yes. The games. Here's what they are so far:

Grease Running—We looked up from our breakfast preparations to see Bubba loping across the campsite, holding aloft a flaming, dripping paper towel. Touchdown-style, she threw it into the fire pit. "If you'd have handed it off to me," yelled Jane, "I could have carried it into the stadium!" The game as it began was the accidental ignition of a grease-soaked paper towel; Bubba correctly reasoned that if she moved fast enough the flames would trail behind her rather than racing up her arm. The game as we now plan it is that the torch is passed from camper to camper until all are ignited. I dunno, think it will catch on?

Soaking—Gather up the dishes and put them into a dishpan with soap, water, and Clorox. Forget about them until the next meal. Not as lively as Grease Running but it has its merits.

Watermelon Seed Wars—Anybody can have a seed-spitting contest. The trick is to spit the seeds at each other so the other campers are covered with the sticky little devils and don't find them all until shower time, when they'll have forgotten about the game and will think they're giant ticks, eeee-yew!

Hot-Wax Dripping—When all is quiet and you're settling in for the night, naked because it's very hot out, you reach over to blow out your nifty little candle lantern, and your sweetie suddenly shrieks at the top of her amazingly powerful lungs. "Well," she explains defensively, "I wasn't expecting hot wax on my bare belly." "We'll make this a tradition," I suggested, "I'll dump hot wax on you the first night of every camping trip."

Potato Dumping—This event happened years ago and is still among our legends. My sweetie was cooking up the best batch of fried potatoes with onion in the history of Dyke Camping (which began in the Cretaceous period). It was late morning after a rowdy night and six of us sat around salivating, awaiting the grand event. She picked up the skillet to dump the potatoes onto a nearby plate, and dumped them onto the ground instead. When she makes the potatoes now, we never forget to ask, "Have these been dumped on the ground yet?" Well, maybe you had to have been there.

Thus starts tradition. You will find your own tribe will grow many of these.

But what we really like best about our campouts is the magic stuff that happens when you're not looking for it.

When you get up at dawn (might as well, can't sleep anyway) and you look over the lake and see a mystical swan creature gliding through the mist on the surface. Or the troglodytes pack up and go home, and you hear the most glorious sounds of all: wind in the trees, bird song, bee buzz, total silence. Or you're going to the smelly outhouse and look up and see a mom woodpecker trying to teach her klutzy offspring to walk up a tree.

Or you're sitting quietly with your coffee during the Soaking event and you realize that being here with your tribe, tired, dirty, silly and smelly, is the best place you could possibly be.

"THE TRIBE" GOES TO A CHORUS FESTIVAL

The Gay and Lesbian chorus festival took place in Tampa, FL, a few years ago. For weeks the chorus had been rehearsing; the small ensemble, Sapphonia, was losing sleep over their most difficult piece, which was something about green thunder, which we groupies have never quite figured out. This is why we are out in front listening and not up there singing. But I digress. We groupies were packing our bags, helping our sweeties remember where they put their music, checking plane schedules and figuring out who was rooming with whom and who was speaking to whom, and is that what the green thunder is really about?

The event itself is a great PR event for gays and lesbians; the mayor of Tampa was amazed at what swell folks we are, even picking up our own trash after the Pride parade Tampa didn't want to give us a permit for. Everyone loved the chorus's performance.

Still, one can only bask in reflected glory so long. "Where's this beach we were promised?" I griped to my sweetie, who also hungered for her ocean fix. Seven of us agreed to spend a day on the Gulf Coast, called a car rental place, and before you could read the *Encyclopedia Britannica* out loud we all piled into our chariot. The *Encyclopedia?* Well, by a supreme accident in judgment, we'd sent Joan and Marty, the two slowest-moving member of the group, to fetch the car. We didn't know they were like this, until then. You know, every couple has one person who can't find her keys or forgot to change her shoes at the last minute, and another person who stands at the door and fumes. Joan and Marty are a bad miracle; both lose their shoes, and both stand there fuming. They just take turns doing it. Sometime after lunch, however, a pink Town Car, a huge thyroidal gas hog if you ever saw one, lumbered into view. "I thought we'd need the biggest thing we could get," explained Joan.

We climbed into this Republican housewife's car, which was bigger on the outside than inside; two of the women are fairly large, one has severe back problems, another has a trick knee, and I'm a hypochondriac who doesn't like to touch people for fear they are bearing germs. Never mind how we did it. Suffice it that we all are much better friends now than we ever intended to be, and all germs proved benign.

By the time we arrived at the Pass-a-grill Beach (we don't know why it's named that but would be glad to entertain theories) it was raining. There's something odd about the human mind, which insists that you take your towel down to the beach even when it's raining and you know that later you'll want a dry towel. We ran into the water and remained there for several hours as the rain poured down and diluted the salt on our faces. It was heaven. I described for Marty, who'd never been to the ocean, the glories of sharks, jellyfish, and rip tides. (We hypochondriacs know these things). She didn't care.

Afterwards, we sat at picnic tables under an awning and dined on fresh fish, loudly pitying the rest of the chorus. My sweetie, who never likes to talk to strangers, wandered up to the table ten minutes after we assembled there, and laconically announced that the motel two doors away had three rooms available, all with kitchens, one overlooking the water, she'd seen that room and it was really neat, should we reserve all three?

I won't elaborate on the remaining days of the six truants from GALA (the seventh truant stayed behind; six dykes with luggage will fit in a Town Car, just) because you'd be so ill with envy that you couldn't stand it.

I won't tell the long story of our being late to dinner one night because Joan and Marty discovered a whole pile of sand dollars in the water, which we pointed out were still living and probably had been interrupted in the throes of passion (thus explaining the odd yellow substance on Joan's fingers) and so of course they had to return all twenty-five of them to exactly where they got them and apologize to the other two they dropped when a wave knocked them over. Or the communal trip to the grocery "for a few things" that resulted in a total bill over $110.00. I won't mention the elaborate communal brunch we prepared and consumed in courses in our room, lingering over coffee and looking out at the waves.

I won't list all the marvelous critters we saw, including Roseate Spoonbills in flight. I will mention that when we returned to the rest of the chorus at the end of the week for a final performance, nearly everyone who'd stayed in town was either ill, in tears, or had broken up with a lover or all three.

We returned home in triumph, sans sand dollars, sunburned, broke, and happy, to find that our cats had upchucked all over the rug and the building contractor had left our kitchen sink leaning against the garage wall. We'll see you all at the next GALA; don't bother cleaning your rugs before you go and be sure to nail down your kitchen sink.

All of these stories, and more, lead to the formation of the first-ever "official" Amazon Girls tribe, the Trailblazers.

AMAZON GIRLS TRAILBLAZER'S TRIBE STOMPS UP?

Those of you who have been closely following developments with the world's first Amazon Girl tribe will be impressed to see that the Trailblazers have already broken with tradition. While the Handbook recommends that a tribe consist of five to eight members, this innovative group has already grown to 11 members, several of whom have said, "Uniform? We don't need no stinkin' uniform!" All are otherwise properly equipped with the minimum equipment for Tomboy (novice) rank; each member has in her possession a copy of the Tomboy Handbook and a suitably garish pink Tomboy badge. (It's just one of those sick "toughen you up" things.)

The tribe has never met with a full membership, preferring to wander into tribal activities in groups of four to five. Tribal activities have included an outdoor movie night at the IMA, an evening at the theater, and a campout that was originally planned as three days at the Dunes campground but ended up being a sleepover with barbecue and hot-tub soak.

Four of the members have met the requirements to Stomp Up to full Amazon Girl status. These are Tomboys who have learned the Amazon Girl oath, salute, ideals, and motto. They have also met some other requirements, such as being able to prepare a meal that is edible, fills up the diners and doesn't make them throw up; correctly identifying two local birds and three wildlife plants, and identifying certain lesbian cultural icons.

The four dedicated Trailblazers convened with due solemnity and performed their ceremony, reciting the oath and ideals, giving the salute, announcing their tribal names, and, of course, dining in grand style and soaking in the hot tub. These Amazon Girls have been awarded their official badges, and two of the four plan to sew them onto their uniform shirts as soon as they find them again.

As you can see, many of the things you're already doing are serious Amazon Girl material, for which you should be awarding yourselves badges, or at least a party to celebrate. So, what are you waiting for?

YOUR LIFE AS AN AMAZON GIRL

Your own conscience and the decisions of your tribe are the guiding principles for how you apply Amazon Girls to your daily life. There is no central organization that tells you how you must behave toward your fellow beings or your planet; Amazon Girls is not a cult.

Unlike certain quasi-military children's organizations, we will not tell you who is eligible to be an Amazon Girl. If some nice boy wants to be an official lesbian and join your tribe, it's up to your tribe and nobody else to decide whether and how to assimilate him. If your tribe wishes to be "womyn-born-womyn-only," that's your prerogative—just remember that you must also deal with the hurt feelings of your trans friends on your own.

Now that you've experienced the joys of Amazon Girl life with your tribe, working toward badges, earning glories and honor, we hope you'll share your wisdom with your fellow lesbians. Feel free to shamelessly proselytize among your non-AG friends. Imagine the glories of lording it over your know-it-all acquaintances as they struggle through Tomboyhood and forget the second Amazon Girl ideal for the third time in a row. Imagine the uproarious parties you can throw as they Stomp Up to full-fledged Amazon Girls. Spread the word.

RESOURCES FOR YOUNG & OLD AMAZON GIRLS

Our Amazon Girls' web page!
www.amazongirls.org

Lambda Legal Defense and Education Fund
www.lambdalegal.org

The P.E.R.S.O.N. Project Home Page
www.youth.org/loco/PERSONProject/

Parents, Families and Friends of Lesbians and Gays
www.pflag.org

GLAAD Gay & Lesbian Alliance Against Defamation
www.glaad.org

GLSEN — Gay, Lesbian, and Straight Education Network
www.glsen.org

Gay Yellow Pages
http://gayellowpages.com

ANNE LEUCK FELDHAUS
STUDIO

PAINTINGS . ILLUSTRATION . PET PORTRAITS

ANNESART.COM

Phone & Fax: 773.772.1085
E-Mail: Anne@AnnesArt.com
Web: www.AnnesArt.com

Wicker Park Press
Chicago